# SUPERGOOD:

## A GUIDE TO
# LIVING IN PURSUIT OF YOUR POTENTIAL

## 30 PRINCIPLES OF SUCCESS

Deanna,

It's been a pleasure working with you.

Have a supergood day!

Best Wishes,

Mike S.

# SUPERGOOD:

## A GUIDE TO
## LIVING IN PURSUIT OF YOUR POTENTIAL

## 30 PRINCIPLES OF SUCCESS

### Written by Mike Swanson

2nd Edition
Copyright © 2008 by Mike Swanson
Edited by Barbara L. Evans
All Rights Reserved
ISBN: 1440498784
EAN-13: 9781440498787

*You can do anything as long as you can visualize it and believe it.*

www.FeelingSuperGood.com

# LIVING IN PURSUIT OF YOUR POTENTIAL
# 30 PRINCIPLES OF SUCCESS

## TABLE OF CONTENTS

# LIVING IN PURSUIT OF YOUR POTENTIAL
## 30 PRINCIPLES OF SUCCESS

This book is about getting what you want out of life.

The good news is that you already have what it takes to achieve your dreams.

The question is: Are you willing to do what is necessary in order to achieve them?
Let this book be your guide for Action.

*Living in Pursuit of your Potential* is a way of life that embraces 30 Principles of Success. Life is about the journey. It is a process. It is about living right now.

It is the *anticipation* of achieving our goals that makes us feel good. Therefore we should always be in pursuit of a greater goal. You always have more Potential.

The 30 Principles will help you achieve the success you seek. If you use these Principles in your life then not only may you find success, but you will enjoy the journey and the process of achieving your dreams.

Many people are looking for the secret to success. You may wonder...
How do I become a success?
How do I become rich?

Ask yourself: If I knew what I needed to do to achieve my dreams, would I do it? Am I willing to pay the price?

If you are able to read this book with an open mind, then you have everything it takes to achieve your goals and live the life of your dreams.

> **This book was designed as a reference guide.**
> **Although presented in a logical order**
> **it is easy to skip around.**

The concepts in this book have been written and rewritten a thousand times by a thousand people in a thousand different ways. When you spend time with rich and successful people that are all 'singing the same song' you begin to realize the truth in this Philosophy.

I first became aware of these Principles several years ago when I began studying real estate investing. I knew that real estate was a path to wealth but I made some surprising discoveries along the way. As I began to meet people that were successful in real estate, I quickly realized that they were all following similar pieces of a collective Philosophy. Many of the rich and successful people I met were all discussing practical philosophies of success as much as they were discussing real estate.

Soon after I began the study of this Philosophy, I made a shift from a neutral attitude to a good one. Every thought or feeling you have can be described as either positive or negative. A central theme of this Philosophy is that negative thoughts and feelings must be eliminated and replaced with positive ones. I decided to start each day feeling *supergood* and it has made all the difference.

There are times in our lives when we must acknowledge and face negativity in order to find ways around it. Negative thoughts should be eliminated, but they must be *replaced, not repressed.* If there is something negative in your life, you must deal with it instead of brushing it under the carpet and ignoring it. Although the Philosophy teaches constant positive thinking, we will be facing some negative topics head on. There are frequently obstacles to cross in the pursuit of your potential and continuous positive living.

I sincerely desire for you to apply these philosophies to your life and see a world that is abundant, wonderful, and full of miracles.

This book is a compilation of theories and principles of success. There are countless ideas for success, many of which can be grouped together or subdivided.

My goal is to summarize the main Principles of Success and explain them as simply and quickly as possible.
I have done my best to do this in 30 chapters.

Many successful people have made outstanding careers with mastery of only *one* of the principles in this book.

As you read, you will undoubtedly say, "I know someone who is rich and successful that doesn't do this." I am sure you do. I can think of a number of people who have achieved great success with the mastery of only one of the concepts in this book.

For this reason, I believe that I can help you. If you learn only *one* new thing from this book, it could be the *one thing* that propels your life to a new place.

I would love to help get you to that new place.

Before we get started, I would like to give credit where credit is due for the source of my inspiration.

In addition to my own experiences I have derived these principles of success by studying the works of the following authors and teachers: Napoleon Hill, Earl Nightingale, Wallace Wattles, Ronda Byrne, Robert Kiyosaki, Bob Proctor, Stephen Covey, Jack Canfield, Greg Pinneo, Dale Carnegie, Dolf De Roos, Mr. Positive David Boufford, T. Harv Eker, Michael Gerber, James Arthur Ray, and others.

Without these teachers, I would not have found the success I currently enjoy and would not have been able to share this Philosophy with you. Please study all their works. Their work is listed at the end of the book for your reference.

If you wish to make further inquiries, feel free to call or email me at 800-360-5914 - www.FeelingSuperGood.com.

## CHAPTER 1 – RESPONSIBILITY

We need to set a foundation.
The foundation is realizing that:

YOU ARE RESPONSIBLE FOR YOUR OWN LIFE.

It is up to you, and only you.
The world does not owe you anything, although it will give back what you give first.

You are responsible for your own actions.
You must accept responsibility for your life.
Your survival and success is your responsibility.
*It all starts with you.*

Your present experience is a result of all the thoughts you've had in the past *and* of all your *responses* to your past experiences.

If you feel victimized, and that the world owes you something, this sentiment should end *now*.
The world is on your side so long as you *believe it is*.

You have a Responsibility in this world, and your rewards will reflect your actions.
It is your Responsibility to choose your path.

Armed with the knowledge in this book, you have no excuses. It is all up to you. Make the choice to take responsibility and we can begin an exciting journey and enjoy the ride.

"Don't go around saying the world owes you a living. The world owes you nothing. It was here first. "
- Mark Twain, 1835-1910

## CHAPTER 2 – YOU GET WHAT YOU GIVE

### You Get what you Give → Every Time.
### ◆ The Golden Rule ◆

This is a precious idea and is by no means a new one. This philosophy has been passed down through the ages for a good reason.

If asked about the Golden Rule many people recall it as: *Treat others as you would like to be treated.*
That is fine and good and true. However, it is the *second* part that is even more important.

***Treat others as you would like to be treated BECAUSE that is how others WILL treat you.***

You will get what you give.

What goes around comes around.

"So in everything, do to others what you would have them do to you…" – Matthew 7:12

In 1905 Albert Einstein gave to the world his now famous discovery that $E=mc^2$. This formula explains the relationship between energy and matter. In the formula: $E$ is energy, $m$ is mass, and $c$ represents the velocity of light. By understanding and applying this formula man has been able to turn matter into energy and energy into matter. Einstein's formula is known as the mass-energy equivalence formula.

We can now see that because matter and energy is the same thing, everything in the universe is related.

If everything in the universe is related then there is a direct cause and effect for everything that happens.

In 1687 Sir Isaac Newton gave to the world his now famous observation that:
"For every action there is an equal and opposite reaction."

Throughout time and many religions we hear the golden rule again and again.

*You will Get what you Give - Every Time.*

There are no accidents and no coincidences. They are merely perceptions of what is happening. Everything is caused by something. Everything you do will cause an equal reaction.

What are you putting out into the universe?
What effects will that have?

Many people abide by the concept of Karma. You are responsible for your own life because the effects of your deeds will cause your future experiences. Your future is the product of each individual choice that you make.

Do good things and good things will happen.
Do bad things and bad things will happen.

*You Get what you Give.*

Given this information, think about how you will change your actions knowing that everything you do will have an equal effect.

If you steal, people will steal from you.
If you cheat, people will cheat you.
If you lie, people will lie to you.

Ponder this: Wouldn't it be better to help other people so that others will help you?

Give to others.  Others will give to you.
Feed others.  Others will feed you.
Care for others.  Others will care for you.
Teach others.  Others will teach you.
Do a little extra.  Get a little extra.

Be a person of Honesty & Integrity.

Be an inspiration to others and they will be an inspiration to you.

Take actions that will make the world a better place and *your world will be a better place.*

At this point, it is pertinent to discuss timing.
The universe is complex, and we have not yet figured out the entire timing of the law of cause and effect.  You do not always see immediate and direct results from what you give or what you put out into the universe.  On a physical level like that which Sir Isaac Newton

described, timing can be measured scientifically. On a karmic or cosmic level, it is much more uncertain and unpredictable.

You may be still paying the price today for some bad actions in the past. You may have *yet* to pay the price for a bad action in the past. Similarly, it may take a while to reap the rewards of your good actions.

A helpful analogy is thinking that every time you act, you are throwing a boomerang into the future. When the boomerang comes back, what will it bring with it? Will it be positive or negative?

The more good you put out, the more good will come back to you.

Let's now address SERVICE. To be successful you must provide SERVICE. Every successful business is serving people. *You* are in the business of serving people. You know that you get what you give; therefore you must consistently provide good Service to others. Great success, especially financially, is achieved by providing excellent quality and quantity of SERVICE.

*Do unto others as you would have them do unto you*
*BECAUSE they will do unto you as you have done unto them.*

## **CHAPTER 3**
## **WHAT YOU KNOW VS. WHAT YOU DON'T KNOW**

You know what you know and you don't know what you don't know. The important *difference* between the two is the concept of *Awareness*.

Think of 2 circles, one inside the other. Like this:

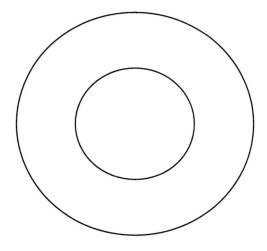

The outer circle represents everything there is to know. The inner circle represents everything that you know.

The perimeter (or edge) of the inner circle represents your AWARENESS of what you don't know.

Wise people acknowledge that they know very little in comparison to all that there is to know.

So realistically, the circles look more like this:

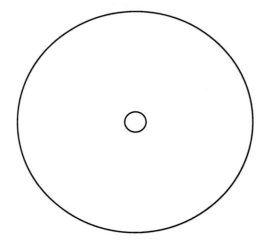

As you learn, the inner circle grows:

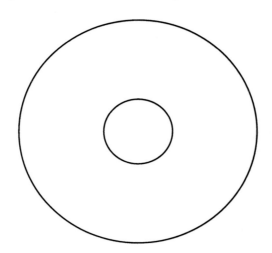

As the inner circle grows, so does your Awareness of that which you don't know.

The more you know, the more you *realize* how much you don't know.

Those with greatest wisdom have the deepest understanding and acknowledgement of their ignorance. They understand the scope of all there still is to know.
The outer circle is very large - Much larger than can be depicted in these diagrams… you get the idea.

Teenagers tend to think they know a lot because their *Awareness* of all that there is to know is *very small*:

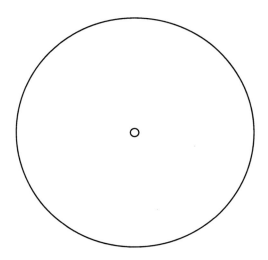

The perimeter of their inner circle – their AWARENESS –is very small.

Now imagine the power of people teaming up and pooling their knowledge. Collectively working together, all involved are able to attain more knowledge.

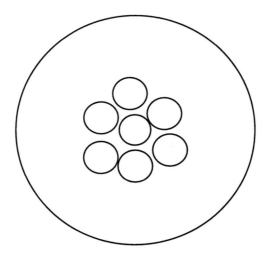

Realistically, most people share some knowledge so the circles overlap and look more like this:

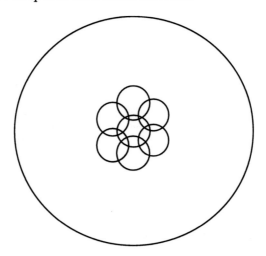

A mother and daughter might look something like this:

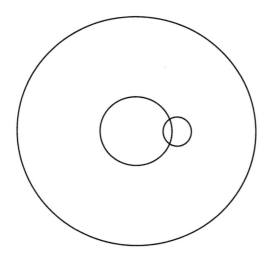

There is some knowledge that they share but even the daughter who is younger and less experienced still has some knowledge that the mother does not. In fact, from the daughters' perspective, the mom does not possess even half of the knowledge that the daughter does.

Understanding what you know and what you don't know is a foundation for success. Be humble and therefore wise; realize that you do not know it all. *Any attempt to increase your knowledge will expand your ignorance.* This is the growth of your Awareness.

Successful people understand these facts and never stop learning. They are wise and therefore make better decisions. While embodying constant growth and movement, wisdom leads to contentment and happiness.

## CHAPTER 4
## THE POWER OF THE SUBCONSCIOUS MIND

The Subconscious Mind is *powerful*.

Most people not only take this concept for granted, but they unknowingly harm themselves with it.

Let's discuss the differences between the Conscious and the Subconscious Mind:

Your Conscious Mind is a wonderful tool that you control to think about whatever you choose to think about. You can use it to focus your thoughts and attention on whatever you choose: you learn, plan, analyze problems and think of solutions. You use your Conscious Mind for a variety of activities on a daily basis.

As you go about your day, whether your thoughts are focused or not, your Conscious Mind is always telling your Subconscious Mind what to believe.

Your Subconscious Mind is working 'behind the scenes' 24-hours-a-day to turn the thoughts of your Conscious Mind into physical reality. Your Subconscious Mind is devoted to making the dominant thoughts of your Conscious Mind come into your life. Your Subconscious Mind is a much better problem solver than your Conscious Mind. Leverage this fact.

As you start to condition your Subconscious Mind in a positive way, you will become more aware of the opportunities around you every day that will bring you closer to your goals.

Just as your Conscious Mind impresses thoughts upon your Subconscious Mind, your Subconscious Mind also influences your Conscious Mind.

Have you ever experienced a 'hunch' or a moment of inspiration?  Have you ever had a 'revelation?'  This is simply your Subconscious Mind communicating with your Conscious Mind.

Most people experience this as a great idea that came out of nowhere, an 'epiphany' if you will.

Imagine this:  You are intently thinking about a particular question or problem, yet are unable to reach a conclusion or solution.  Feeling exhausted you decide to go to bed and leave the problem for later.  Then behold, the answer comes to you in the morning.

This is a fairly common experience that happens as a result of your Subconscious Mind working non-stop even when (and especially when) you are sleeping.

Your Subconscious Mind is controlled by your thought patterns.  Your Subconscious Mind believes anything believed by your Conscious Mind.

If you know that you can fix a problem, or change an unwanted situation then you *can…* thanks to your Subconscious Mind.  As long as you *truly believe* you can do something, your Subconscious Mind will believe it as well!

The tricky part is that since your Subconscious Mind is such a great problem solver, you want to be careful what problems you start having it solve.

Your Subconscious Mind cannot tell the difference between what is true and what is not. Although this is tremendous opportunity, it can be damaging if not properly guided.

Unfortunately, many people think negative thoughts with their Conscious Mind. This causes the Subconscious Mind to seek more negativity. Negative thinking attracts negative people and experiences. Positive thinking attracts positive people and experiences.

We often rely on our Conscious Minds to tell us what is true and false. Unfortunately, our Conscious Minds are not always accurate in their assessment of a situation. This can sometimes cause improper actions or reactions.

A common mistake is the perception that 'seeing is believing'. Our eyes *often* deceive us if we rely *only* on our Conscious Mind to interpret what we see. Many people interpret what they see as fact and draw a conclusion based on those facts. This appears to be solid reasoning until we consider the possibility that 'something other than what we saw actually happened.'

Your Subconscious Mind cannot determine what is real. It sees everything as real. It relies on your Conscious Mind to assign value and truth.

What are you telling your Subconscious Mind?

Here is what many people are telling their Subconscious Minds. Do *you* have these thoughts or questions?

- Work sucks.
- I hate my boss.
- I can't afford it.
- I need more money.
- Life isn't fair.
- Why can't I catch a break?
- How will I get out of debt?
- Why am I always sick?
- Why is life so hard?

Many people have a tendency to focus on the negative. They think about their problems, worries, and fears. As a result, these things are attracted and thus *repeatedly experienced.*

Your Subconscious Mind creates the physical manifestation of what your Conscious Mind believes and focuses on. Your Subconscious Mind works to bring the thoughts of your Conscious Mind to physical reality.

If you tell yourself that you are not good enough, your Mind will work to make sure that you are never good enough. If you tell yourself that you are old, your Mind will work to make sure that you feel, look and act old.

Successful people feed their Subconscious Mind with proactive and empowering thoughts and questions:

- I feel great
- I look great
- I feel healthy
- I am thankful and grateful for what I have.
- People are generous and kind.
- There is always opportunity.
- What do I want?  What are my goals?
- What am I going to do to obtain them?

Be mindful of what you tell yourself because your Subconscious Mind will start working to make your dominant thoughts *a reality*.

How to communicate with your Subconscious Mind:

1. Be clear and sure of what you are thinking, the Subconscious Mind likes messages in their simplest form.
2. Do not dwell on negativity.  Your Subconscious Mind will pick up on it and grow it rather than conquer it.
3. Be Positive.  It is easy to stay on the right path with positive messages to your subconscious.
4. Your Subconscious Mind is especially impressionable right before bed and just as you wake up.  Think positive thoughts and tell yourself positive motivating messages all day, but especially during these particular times of day.

5. Communicate positive messages to your subconscious with *Emotion, Passion, and Conviction* and challenge yourself to truly mean what you are telling yourself.

For Example:

**Do not say:** I want to quit smoking.

Your Subconscious Mind hears: 'Want, Quit, & Smoking' and it will work to create those things in your life: A feeling of want, a desire to quit, and a need to smoke.

**Instead say:** I enjoy breathing clean air.

Your Subconscious Mind hears: 'Joy, Breathing & Clean Air' and it will work to create those things in your life: A feeling of joy, the ability to breathe, and clean air.

**Do not say:** I want to get out of debt.

Your Subconscious Mind hears: 'Want & Debt' and it will work to create those things in your life.

**Instead say:** I am good with my money.

Your Subconscious Mind hears: 'Good & Money' and it will work to create those things in your life.

**Do not say:** I want to lose weight.

Your Subconscious Mind hears: 'Want, Lose & Weight' and it will work to create those things in your life.

**Instead say:** I am fit and healthy.

Your Subconscious Mind hears: 'Fit & Healthy' and it will work to create those things in your life.

Do you see the pattern?

What are you telling yourself?

What are you telling your Subconscious Mind?

Thinking the same thoughts repeatedly and with great emotion impresses them into your Subconscious Mind. Thoughts with great emotion and conviction will be picked up more quickly than emotionless thoughts. Your Subconscious Mind weights your thoughts based on the strength of the feelings connected with them.

*Feel* what you wish your subconscious to comprehend. Believing something with *great emotion* impresses your Subconscious Mind more than repetition alone.

Do you ever think negative thoughts with great emotion?

Undoubtedly you have felt feelings of Fear, Doubt, Jealousy, Hatred, Anger, Revenge, or Resentment. These feelings are usually felt with *strong emotion*. The strength of these emotions causes these negative thoughts to be quickly absorbed by the Subconscious Mind.

At this point you should understand that it is a disaster to let negative emotions such as Fear, Doubt, Worry, Anger, Jealousy, Revenge or Resentment seep into your Subconscious Mind.

Do you want your Subconscious Mind spending time figuring out how to attract negative things into your life? Certainly it makes more sense to feed your Subconscious Mind thoughts of your positive future goals. Keep your Subconscious Mind busy with positive thoughts of your future achievements.

When you feel negative emotions, turn them into something positive.  Think of your goals and dreams and focus on those instead.  Keep your thoughts positive and optimistic.  Thoughts of your goals should make you feel good.

You have a responsibility to program your own Mind.  If you do not program your Mind, your environment and those around you will program it for you.

Now that we have discussed your Subconscious Mind, you should realize that worrying is not only useless but also extremely damaging.  Worrying creates a situation in which your Subconscious Mind turns your worries into physical realities.  *Do not worry.*  In the next chapter you will gain a greater understanding of the dangers of worrying.

Use your Subconscious Mind for Good: what you think about will happen to you.

## CHAPTER 5
## YOU WILL BECOME WHAT YOU THINK ABOUT

You are the result of every thought you have ever had.
Collectively, your thoughts have made you who you are.

If you want to change your life, change your thoughts.

"As a man thinks in his heart, so is he."-Proverbs 23: 7

Although you will become what you think about, it is
fortunate that you cannot just think of something and
make it appear. It would be a chaotic world if this were
the case.

There is more to it than this. Your thoughts become
reality with the help of the Subconscious Mind based on
the frequency, repetition, *emotion* and conviction of your
thoughts. Your Mind addresses your thoughts in ways
that are subtle. Be open to the fact that this contact comes
in various forms. Your Subconscious Mind is frequently
trying to communicate to you the same ideas again and
again. You must be receptive. Do not ignore your
intuition.

You may have heard or read before that 'you are a
product of the things you read and the people you spend
time with.' It is true that you tend to become a product
of your environment because *you will become what you
think about.*

As you read books and other forms of literature, you
think about what you are reading. You cannot avoid
thinking about it because you have to mentally process it.
Your Mind translates the letters on the page into

something meaningful. Reading is an excellent way to feed your Mind - be mindful of what you feed it.

When you spend time with your friends, family and co-workers you become a product of their thinking and vice versa. They begin to think like you and you begin to think like them. Challenge yourself to be a positive and spirited addition to this collective thinking.

Once people truly realize the influence the people they spend time with have on their lives, many will make changes in the company they keep. Think about the influences that the people you surround yourself with have in your life. Are they positive?

In order to achieve success, you may need to re-evaluate others' influences in your life. Do you have a close family member or friend who is frequently negative?

Their influence in your life *must be reduced*. It may sound harsh, but it is the truth.

"Be careful the environment you choose for it will shape you; be careful the friends you choose for you will become like them." -W. Clement Stone, 1902-2002

Negative people, whether family, friends or strangers must be kept at a distance. Do not let their thoughts become your thoughts.

Evaluate the thoughts you hold in your head.

Are they empowering thoughts? Are they thoughts of your positive goals? Are they thoughts of your future achievements? Are they positive and good for you? Or are they negative and harmful?

People spend a lot of time watching TV, playing video games, or gossiping. Just remember that you will become what you think about. Be careful how you spend your time and be careful what you put in your Mind.

Negative thinking is a disaster. As you begin to realize and believe that *you become what you think about*, you will realize that the negative thoughts of doubt, hatred, fear, anger, jealousy, revenge, and resentment must disappear.

These emotions will hurt you because they are negative. Do not attract these negative feelings into your life.

Instead of being 'your own worst enemy,' try being your own best friend!

**Forgiveness will free your Mind.**

Forgive every person who has ever hurt you in any way. You cannot afford to keep this negative energy in your life.

My favorite definition of forgiveness is: being able to tell the person who wronged you, "thank you for that experience."

Forgive everyone; otherwise the experience you had with them may be still harming you to this day. It will continue to harm you until you forgive.

## AN IMPORTANT METAPHOR:

### Your Mind is a Garden.

> Your Mind is a garden of rich soil that will grow whatever you plant and nurture.  The choice is yours.  You can grow absolutely anything you want so long as you tend to it.  Like a garden, your Mind does not care what you plant.  Plant anything you like and it will grow.  Plant roses, roses will grow.  Plant corn, corn will grow.  Plant briars or blackberries and they will grow as well.
>
> Note that you do not have to nurture or plant the weeds.  They plant themselves.  Like weeds, negative thoughts sprout up where they are unwanted.  You must keep the weeds under control.
>
> You must plant the things you want to grow, and keep the things you don't want out.  Spend your time growing your garden.  Feed your Mind with the good stuff and keep the bad stuff out.  Your Mind is a garden.

You have complete control over your Mind.
Do not let it go to waste.
Use it to create whatever you want.

I encourage asking yourself: What am I growing in my garden?

*If you can believe it, you can achieve it, so long as you set it as your goal and visualize it on a regular basis.*

What are your goals? Are you currently nurturing what you want to grow in your life, or are you allowing weeds to inundate?

"The thing always happens that you really believe in; and the belief in a thing makes it happen."
-Frank Lloyd Wright

"You see, you can do anything if you put your focus on how to do it rather than on why you can't."
-Bob Proctor

"There is a law in psychology that if you form a picture in your Mind of what you would like to be, and you keep and hold that picture there long enough, you will soon become exactly as you have been thinking."
-William James, 1842-1910

"Man alone has the power to transform his thoughts into physical reality; man alone can dream and make his dreams come true." -Napoleon Hill, 1883-1970

"If you can dream it, you can do it."
-Walt Disney, 1901-1966

"All that we are is the result of what we have thought."
-Buddha, 400BC

*You will become what you think about.*

## CHAPTER 6 – THE IMPORTANCE OF GOALS

Earl Nightingale defines success as "The progressive realization of a worthy goal".

How can you be a success without goals?
**You must know where you are going if you ever intend to get there. How are you going to reach your destination if you do not know where it is?**
Set your goals and think of them often.
Many people do not have goals. Of the people who *have* set goals, only a few have written them down. If you do not have goals written down on a piece of paper in a visible place, you need to do so *now*.

Your goals should be *positive* and make you feel good when you think about them.

Write down your goals. Do it *now*.

When you write down your goals, you better impress them upon your Subconscious Mind. As a result, you will begin to take subconscious actions toward their attainment. These subconscious actions will move you toward conscious and tangible results. Write your goals down and read them out loud. Repeat this process often and do it with *emotion and passion*.

You must also *believe* your goal is achievable and *know* that you will reach it. If you do not believe that you can achieve a goal then you almost certainly will not. If you truly believe you *can* achieve your goals, you most certainly *will!* One thing I recommend for reinforcing belief in your goals is to share them with others with full Faith and confidence that they will be achieved. This allows your subconscious to get used to them as inevitabilities, rather than just leaving them as mere possibilities. Sharing your goals also helps to hold yourself accountable for them.

Inspired from Earl Nightingale, I would like to share what I call *Boat Theory*. Imagine that people are boats.

Boats have a motor and a rudder. The motor is your ability and desire to take Action. The rudder is your ability to steer your Action in a direction.

- Many people do not use either their motor or their rudder. They just bob along and go where the wind and currents take them; they believe they are a victim of circumstance and that they do not get anywhere because the world won't 'give them a break.' Chances are, they will crash or sink before they reach any worthy destination. They are just bobbing along aimlessly allowing the elements to take their toll.
- Some people take a lot of action and race along at full speed. However, if they have no goal or destination in mind then they are really just going nowhere fast. Those who may appear successful and busy are not necessarily living the life of their dreams.
- Other people have a rudder that is fixed in a certain position causing them to go around in circles. Whether they are going fast or slow, they are still going around in circles. If they are focused on anything, it is usually the same thing day after day.

- Some people have charted a course, know where they are going, have a hand on the rudder, and move forward at a steady pace. These are the truly successful people. They have a goal, take action toward it, and keep the ship headed in the right direction until they reach their final destination.

Which kind of boat are you?

"Desire is the starting point of all achievement, not a hope, not a wish, but a keen pulsating Desire which transcends everything." -Napoleon Hill

In order to ensure that your goal will be achieved, it must be more than just a wish or a dream. You must solidify it in your Mind and convince yourself that you have already achieved it (just not yet). Your goal must not only be written down where you can see it daily, it must be visualized and crystallized into a burning desire.

Napoleon Hill refers to your goal as your "Definite Chief Aim". Your Subconscious Mind must be clear about the objective. Sometimes having multiple goals can dilute the focus of your Subconscious Mind. Make sure that your goals are simple, clear and defined.

Stephen Covey's 2nd Habit is "Begin with the End in Mind". This means that you need a goal. You need to know where you are going so that you can visualize it.

Goal setting is the time for you to make a choice.

Decide what you shall set your heart upon and go for it! Set your Heart and Mind on what you want and *go get it!*

"My philosophy of life is that if we make up our mind what we are going to make of our lives, then work hard toward that goal, we never lose - somehow we win out." -Ronald Reagan, 1911-2004

### VISUALIZATION

Visualization is a technique that will help solidify your goals into your Subconscious Mind.

As you visualize, you must take yourself to the place you want to go. Picture the details; imagine the sights, sounds, smells and textures.

How do you visualize your future?

"Dream lofty dreams and as you dream so shall you become" –Goethe, 1749-1832

"You need to say you're there before you're there in order to get there." – Greg Pinneo

If you visualize your goal and immerse yourself in it as if it is already a reality, chances are, you will achieve it.

Visualizing and embracing your goal will impress it upon your Subconscious Mind.

***PLEASE* - DO NOT START THE NEXT CHAPTER WITHOUT WRITING DOWN AT LEAST ONE GOAL.**

"If you know what to do to reach your goal, it's not a big enough goal." -Bob Proctor

*Write your goals down where you can see them daily.* Try to find a photo of your goals for better visualization. Place a picture of your goal where you can see it daily. Visualize it frequently.

IF YOU WISH, YOU CAN WRITE SOME OF YOUR GOALS HERE:

## CHAPTER 7 – AFFIRMATIONS

Affirmations are an implementation technique for your goals.

Similar to goals, Affirmations help your Subconscious Mind understand where you are heading.

Since we know that you will become what you think about, make your thoughts positive and affirming.

You will believe whatever you repeatedly tell yourself.

Anything you tell yourself repeatedly and with great emotion *will* become your reality. While this is true, it does not always have positive outcomes. For example, a person who constantly thinks of revenge and violence is bound to hurt someone. A person who constantly thinks about happiness will likely be happy.

Do you remember the story of the "little engine that could?" The little engine kept repeating the phrase "I think I can, I think I can," until he successfully reached the top of the hill.

This story teaches the importance of having a goal and believing in yourself. It also illustrates that the repetition of an affirmation helps to create its reality.

"To be a great champion you must believe you are the best. If you're not, pretend you are." -Muhammad Ali

Write down some empowering positive thoughts about your future goals and repeat them with emotion and passion frequently.

For example:

- I am happy and healthy.
- I believe in myself and my ability to achieve my goals.
- I believe in my friends, family and co-workers.
- I am good with money.
- I am on my way to realizing [My Goal].
- I look at the positive side of everything and make my optimism come true.
- I think only of the best and expect only the best.

It is best to begin an Affirmation with,
"I am thankful and grateful that…"

- I am thankful and grateful that I am happy and healthy.
- I am thankful and grateful that I am good with money.
- I am thankful that I am on my way to realizing [My Goal].

*I will further discuss the importance of being Thankful and Grateful in a later chapter.

## **CHAPTER 8 –REALITY BUBBLES**

Communicating well with others is an essential attribute of success. Throughout the day we send and receive thousands of communications with those around us – both verbally and non-verbally.

During my management career, I had the opportunity to supervise thousands of people, and interact, one-on-one, with many thousands more. This theory evolved from those experiences. Reality Bubbles is a concept about how our perceptions affect our interaction with each other.

Here is a model I used to teach managers effective communication:

Sender ⇨ Message ⇨ Medium ⇨Receiver

The sender sends their message through a medium to a receiver. The sender has something to say. They decide how to say it and send it; then the receiver interprets the message. Although the model is simple, there inevitably exists a potential for the message to be lost or scrambled along the way.

The sender and receiver each have different responsibilities in the communication process. For the most part, *the sender must take responsibility* for the message that is received. The sender must ensure the message arrives properly.

Let's take this concept of communication a step further and think of more than just receiving a message.

Think of the perceptions you have of your experiences throughout the day.

People experience things differently.

Each person has their own interpretation of the world around them.  Each person has their own perception of what is happening.

OUR PERCEPTIONS ARE OUR REALITIES.

Everyone experiences his or her own reality.

We all live in our own reality bubble.

We are all products of our experiences.

Some people believe the same things, so their reality bubbles intersect.  They share a portion of their bubble.

Two close friends who have shared many experiences and hold the same beliefs will share a large portion of their reality bubble.

Two total strangers who are both part of the same business association likely share a portion of their reality bubble even though they have never met.

Two people living on opposite ends of the Earth who speak different languages share a much smaller portion of their reality bubbles.  Even though they are very different they still share some similar experiences such as sunrises, sunsets, emotions, life and death.

Trying to communicate with someone in an entirely different reality bubble may prove challenging.  You are going to need to have some understanding of their reality bubble before you will have a successful communication.

*There is no one reality. We all have our own.*
We create it based on our perceptions and experiences.

The good news is that we can use this concept to create the life of our dreams. We can invent our own reality by changing our beliefs.

Everyone is trying to make sense of the world in which we live based on a limited Awareness and an incomplete picture of what is really happening.

Understanding the fact that our perceptions are our realities will make it easier for you to understand other people. If you can reach inside the reality bubbles of others then you will be an effective communicator.

If you are effective at understanding other people, there will be no need for them to try to understand you.

The ability to negotiate is much easier with an understanding of Reality Bubbles. Understand that your awareness of reality bubbles will aid in your negotiations. Understanding others will greatly improve your communication with them. When you properly understand the reality of others, you can frame your communication in a way that will be best understood.

Here are a few things that are part of my reality bubble, and are hopefully a part of yours now as well:

- The Principles of Success are true and they work.
- I am 100% responsible for my own life.
- The world owes me nothing but the universe will return what I give.
- Life does not play favorites.
- The Law of Cause and Effect is present in everything.
- My Subconscious Mind is more powerful that my Conscious Mind.
- What I think about consistently and with great emotion will happen.
- I have goals.
- I will attract what I think about.
- My results correspond with my attitude.
- Thinking is fun and fruitful.
- The world is abundant.
- God is abundant.
- Efficiency is a result of organization.
- Having a solid plan increases my chance of success.
- When faced with a problem I must make a decision and take Action.
- Fear hinders Action. I Act in spite of Fear.
- A new habit requires decision, determination, and discipline.
- Any success must pass the test of Persistence.
- I have Faith in myself.
- I am thankful and grateful for all that I have.

- I am feeling *Supergood* and happy to be alive.
- I have healthy habits.
- I am tolerant and accepting of others.
- I am too busy improving myself to have time to criticize others.
- I Trust myself and others.
- I Live Deliberately.
- I am constantly learning and growing.
- Everything I do has a consequence.

"It's not what you look at that matters, it's what you see." -Henry David Thoreau, 1817-1862

"I am realistic - I expect miracles." -Wayne Dyer

Define your reality and your Subconscious Mind will work non-stop to make it so. Submit your desires to your Subconscious Mind through Affirmations and your goals and dreams will come true.

## CHAPTER 9 – THE LAW OF ATTRACTION

Ronda Byrne's movie *The Secret* adequately explains the Law of Attraction. This law is another reason why *you become what you think about.*

Simply put, *like attracts like.*

Understanding the power of the Subconscious Mind makes the Law of Attraction much easier to understand and apply.

We are all radiating energy. What type of energy are you sending out? You will attract the same.

In the movie *The Secret*, the Emotional Guidance System is discussed. This is an innate (inborn) system in each of us that helps to guide our thoughts and actions.

Controlling your thoughts every moment of the day is very challenging. Our Emotional Guidance System is here to help guide our thoughts and actions.

If you are not feeling good, then change your thoughts. A good alternative to any negative thought is *Your Goal.* Your goal should be a good positive image of where you want to be and should make you *feel good.*

Take a look at this simple model from T. Harv Eker:

**Thoughts ⇨ Feelings ⇨ Actions ⇨ Results**

Your thoughts cause certain feelings, which prompt certain actions, which yield certain results.

*If you don't like your results, change your thoughts.*

Your thoughts become your words, your words become your actions, and your actions become your reality.
Changing your thoughts will change your results.

In every situation you have ***Response-Ability***. You can respond to any situation in any way you choose. Your responses are usually a result of how you feel. Be careful of your responses for they will affect your future results. Think about the outcomes you desire when choosing your responses to situations and those around you. The nature of your thought will create your results.

"The Law of Attraction attracts to you everything you need, according to the nature of your thought. Your environment and financial condition are the perfect reflection of your habitual thinking. Thought rules the world." -Dr. Joseph Edward Murphy, Surgeon

"You are a human magnet and you are constantly attracting to you people whose characters harmonize with your own." – Napoleon Hill, 1883-1970

## CHAPTER 10 – ATTITUDE

Earl Nightingale calls it the magic word.

"It is our attitude at the beginning of a difficult task which, more than anything else, will affect its successful outcome." –William James, 1842-1910

If you believe you can do it, then you can.
If you do not believe you can do it, then you cannot.

"Whether you think you can or think you can't, you're right either way." – Henry Ford, 1863-1947

It is pretty simple really:
**Your attitude equals your results.**
Great attitude = Great results
Fair attitude = Fair results
Poor attitude = Poor results

It is easy to say, "Keep a positive attitude," but how do you do it?

Please allow me to share a personal experience...
I used to think my attitude was fine. If you asked how I was doing I probably would have told you "fine". I was doing fine and things were going fine. I never thought that I had a bad attitude so whenever people spoke about keeping a good attitude, I did not worry about it. My attitude was fine.

What I did not realize was that my attitude was actually *neutral*. It was not bad but it wasn't necessarily good. It was just fine.

My neutral attitude made it too easy for others to affect my attitude. I would never start the day feeling negative. In fact, in the mornings I usually felt pretty good. I would start out the day feeling fine. What I did not realize is that my neutral attitude often allowed others to bring me down. Their negative attitudes affected me and would often bring me down by mid-day. A neutral attitude is not a good attitude.

I now understand that I need to start the day with more Positive Momentum. If I want to be good all day, I need to start the day feeling *supergood*. That way I will be able to better deflect any negativity. Any negativity that is absorbed will bring me down to a level that is *still good*!

From that point on, I have been *supergood*. Why would anyone want to be any other way?

If other people are having a bad day, it is *their* problem. Not yours. You are good no matter what. While it may not be your problem, you should always take the opportunity to positively affect those who are having a bad day. Remember that you get what you give, so you should always be helping others.

"If you don't like something, change it. If you can't change it, change your attitude. Don't complain."
-Maya Angelou

In every situation you have two choices: you can be positive or negative. The choice is yours.

Take responsibility and be Positive.

Once your Subconscious Mind adopts the habit of being genuinely positive, this habit will soon be reflected in your results.

Think of someone you know who is upbeat and positive. How do you feel when you are around them?

Think of someone you know who is generally negative. How do you feel when you are around them?

Attitudes are contagious. This is why you want to be careful who you spend time with.

For the best presentation on Attitude please listen to Earl Nightingale's *Lead the Field*.

"Nothing can stop the man with the right mental attitude from achieving his goal; nothing on earth can help the man with the wrong mental attitude."
-Thomas Jefferson, 3rd U.S. President, 1743-1826

"The greatest discovery of my generation is that man can alter his life simply by altering his attitude of mind."
-William James, 1842-1910

"For myself, I am an optimist - it does not seem to be much use being anything else. "
-Winston Churchill, 1874-1965

## CHAPTER 11 – USE YOUR MIND AND THINK

Put your Mind to work and think of ways to achieve your Goals. Use your imagination and be creative. If you concentrate your Conscious Mind on a particular problem or goal, your Subconscious Mind will concentrate on it as well. Keep these two forces moving together and you will produce some great new ideas.

I am embarrassed to admit that for a long time I held the belief that most people are 'stupid'. We certainly see a lot of people do a lot of stupid things.

I have realized that people are not stupid. They mostly just *do not think*. Instead they conform. They do what everyone else is doing and don't even know why.

Some people go to great lengths to avoid thinking, and in our culture, this is easy to do. Many people will ask the advice of a total stranger before making an attempt to think and apply their Conscious Mind.

For many people, thinking is not required so they get out of the habit of it. They get up in the morning and they get ready, they go to work and do what their boss tells them. When they get home they eat, or do chores or do what their spouse tells them to do, then they relax, watch a little TV and go to bed.

The process is repeated the next day.

Little independent thought is required.

If a problem arises, many people will either ask someone for advice, or hire a professional to solve it for them.

How *should* we solve problems? Use your Conscious Mind to impress the problem upon your Subconscious Mind in the form of a Positive Affirmation.

With practice you can leverage the intercommunication between your Conscious and Subconscious Mind.

'Necessity is the Mother of Invention'. This is because the Conscious Mind becomes consumed by the particular need. This stimulates the Subconscious Mind to focus on that necessity as well. The emotion of the necessity adds greater power to the Subconscious Mind. Many people will not come up with a new idea until a circumstance requires it.

Those who apply themselves and *think* will more frequently develop great new ideas all of the time, not just when a situation demands it.

The Subconscious Mind is survival oriented by default. Food, water and shelter will always be concerns to your Subconscious Mind. If those are causes of concern in your life then your Subconscious Mind will spend more time working on them.

People are more productive members of society when food, water and shelter become less of a concern. I never recommend taking things for granted, but when you do not need to devote subconscious thinking time to the basics you can start to achieve greater things.

You will achieve what you set out to achieve. If you set out for food you will find it. If you set out for shelter you will find it. If those are your only goals then that is as far as you will get. Think big and seek greater things.

"Ask, and it will be given you, seek, and you will find; knock, and it will be open to you." – Jesus, Matthew 7:7

You need to *Think Bigger*.

Why wish for a loaf of bread?  Why not a whole grocery store?  Why limit yourself?

"If you're going to think anyway, you may as well think big." – Donald Trump.

What is thinking bigger?  Think of the circle diagrams in the chapter about Awareness.  What you know is contained in the inner circle.  Expand that circle.  Think bigger.  Increasing your Awareness of what is around you will help you see new possibilities.  This is thinking bigger.

Study your field of work.  Study all sides of the issues.  Look at all points of view.  Think bigger.

Think back to Boat Theory in the chapter about goals.  Most people have set their rudder so that their boat is going around in a large circle.  They go around and around.  Maybe their circle is big enough that they don't quite realize that they are just going around and around.  Expand your circle.

It is good to use your imagination.  Imagination indicates that your Subconscious Mind is actively communicating with your Conscious Mind.  New ideas bubble up and ideas pop into your head.  Imagination is a good thing.  It is capable of solving great problems.  Creativity adds value to the world.

Think of what you want, set your goal, and get your imagination flowing.  Live now but also keep your Mind on the future.

"Live out of your imagination, not your history."
-Stephen Covey

## CHAPTER 12 – ABUNDANCE VS SCARCITY

There are two ways to live your life. One is a life of abundance and the other is a life of scarcity. The good news is that *you get to choose* which life you want to live.

Many people choose scarcity. They believe that there are a fixed amount of resources on the planet. With this line of thinking, if you have something then someone else will not. Therefore, the rich are viewed as greedy since they are taking something that someone else could have. This *scarcity-minded* thinking and it is *flawed*.

Scarcity is a mindset that must be overcome in order to achieve wealth.

If you believe that in order to get rich you need to deprive someone else of something, then you will not get rich. Your Subconscious Mind will not allow it.

T. Harv Eker's teachings discuss the concept of your "Wealth Blueprint". These are beliefs held in your Subconscious Mind that help or hinder your future progress. You need to adjust your beliefs in order to achieve the life of your dreams.

The world is abundant. The Universe is abundant. God is abundant.
Adapt your thinking toward Abundance.

## **CHAPTER 13 – ORGANIZATION**

Clean up your messes and free your Mind!

I originally intended to call this chapter 'Messes' but messes are not a principle of success. Messes are a hindrance to success.

Your Mind keeps a catalog of everything you own. Every mess is clogging up your Mind. You know you need to clean the garage, clean out the closet, clean your desk, clean your car, clean out the junk drawer, clean out the shed or whatever other mess you may have. They are all blocking the road to success!

What is the point in having something if you cannot find it? How much of your life do you want to spend looking for things you've lost?

Get rid of the messes.

Here is the great part (it's a 2 for 1 deal): Clean up your messes and give the things you don't use to charity. You can clean *and give* at the same time.

Again, your Mind keeps a catalog of everything you own. Junk and messes are clogging up your Mind and hindering your success. Your subconscious is aware of your messes…eliminate them!

The human Mind dwells on incomplete tasks.  Your Mind continues to take you back to incomplete projects.  Your Mind dwells on your messes.
Remove them and free your Mind.

Make a habit of cleaning up one new thing each month.  Make it a goal.  Put in on the calendar.  Put it in your planner.  Remember: put your goals in writing.
Which mess will be this month's challenge?  Which mess will be next month's prize?  The desk?  The garage?  The car?

As you eliminate messes they should be replaced by an organizational system to prevent the mess from reoccurring.

If most of the mess was trash then devise a system or process to prevent the trash from piling up.  If some of the mess is not trash then what is it?  *Why do you have it* and how did it end up becoming a mess?
If it is important enough to keep around, it should be important enough to have a system to manage it.

There are many different clutter management systems.  You may use a filing system to clean up your desk.  You may use color coded baskets to clean up your laundry.  There are many organizational systems available.
However you go about organization, you need the discipline to form a habit to keep the system working.

You can organize a new filing system but if the papers continue to pile up on your desk, you have not conquered your mess.

As you clean up your messes you may tend to 'brush some things under the carpet.' You may condense the mess that is your kitchen into a mess that is now contained in a drawer. Although these steps may reduce one mess, they still create another. I applaud you if you are able to reduce a messy garage to just a couple of messy drawers. However, those drawers need to be the next project.

Don't repress your mess.

Deal with it. Take care of it. Conquer it.

Get organized and get on with your life.

Most importantly: *Clean your messes to free your Mind.*

Use the note space at the back of the book to write down all the messes in your life that need your attention. Assign a realistic date when you will have each of them cleaned up. Choose a mess each month. Cross them off as you eliminate them.

## CHAPTER 14 – PREPARATION

In order to be a success you need to take Action. Action requires Preparation. Preparation is both physical and mental.

Achieving a goal is like climbing a mountain.

Climbing a mountain requires both physical and mental preparation. You need to be *physically* capable of climbing the mountain. Your legs and cardiovascular system must be strong. Your heart and lungs must be able to withstand the strain. Larger mountains will take even greater levels of physical endurance.

Not only must you be physically prepared, you must also be *mentally* prepared. You must be knowledgeable of the terrain, the route and the hazards. You must be knowledgeable of safety procedures and techniques. You must know what to do in case of emergency.

Being prepared reduces the risk associated with any action. You need the right tools for the job, and must know how to use them. You can endanger yourself or others if you take action without the proper equipment and training.

Preparation is needed to achieve your goals, whether it is climbing a mountain or any other pursuit.

Practice is Part of your Preparation.

Assess your goals and decide what type of plan is needed.

- **Your preparation should include a financial plan.** Whether it is the family finances or yours alone, you need some financial goals and a plan to attain them. Track your expenses and monitor them monthly.
- **Your preparation should include a MARKETING plan.** This may be your business marketing plan or your personal marketing plan. Your personal salesmanship of service can dramatically increase your success. In order to achieve great success you must not only take Action but also sell yourself and your ideas to others. This is *marketing*. Everything you do represents the salesmanship of yourself. Either you are promoting yourself or you are not. You may think that you do not need to promote yourself. Not only do you need to, *you already are.* You are telling the world about yourself by the way you look, act, and speak. Promote and present yourself in a way that attracts people who will help you achieve your goals.
- **Your preparation should include a business plan.** If you do not own a business you should consider the possibility. A lot of hobbies would make a good foundation for a new business. Doing something you are passionate about and enjoy dramatically increases your chance of success.

## **CHAPTER 15 – ACTION**

Action is the *core principle.*
Without action, nothing will happen.

Some people succeed using only this principle. They take Action and do so consistently. They are constantly moving and looking for new opportunities.

Action is a pre-requisite for success. It will take a lot of Action and initiative to achieve your goals.

You may have heard it said that "You can't steer a parked car." This is the perfect quote for the person who is prepared but yet does not push forward and take the next step.
"You can't steer a parked car." You have to get it rolling. Once you have read the car manual and studied the traffic laws, you are ready ⇨ Go.

Many people on their way to success get stuck in 'analysis paralysis.' This is the common term for the person who is stuck in the preparation phase and is having trouble moving to the Action phase. *If you are ready then go.*

Once you are prepared, *do not hesitate.*

"The difference between getting somewhere and nowhere is the courage to make an early start. The fellow who sits still and does just what he is told will never be told to do big things." -Charles M. Schwab, 1862-1939

Action is the result of Decision. You must make the Decision to take Action. Becoming more decisive takes faith and practice. As you make decisions more quickly you will gain confidence. This confidence will help you make quick, definite decisions in the future. Trust your intuition.

Great leaders make good decisions quickly.

"Using the power of decision gives you the capacity to get past any excuse to change any and every part of your life in an instant."-Anthony Robbins

Doing *something* is better than doing *nothing*.

"Look for your choices, pick the best one, then go with it."
-Pat Riley

Your gut instinct accounts for a lot. Follow your intuition.

Remember every time you are in a moment of hesitation: *The universe likes speed.* The universe rewards speed. Make decisions quickly and take Action. *Do it now.*

"You can't accomplish anything worthwhile if you inhibit yourself. If life teaches you nothing else, know this for sure: When you get the chance, go for it." -Oprah Winfrey

Action includes follow through. You can set things in motion but you must actively follow-up to make sure things are going as planned.

Each day you must physically do something to get closer to your goal. Be very conscious about your plans once you are in motion. You need to reevaluate your plans, follow up and make sure you stay on course.  Are you sticking to the plan?  Are you adjusting the plan?

Make sure to stick to your initiated Marketing plan.  All existing plans require your attention on an ongoing basis.
Define your goals then take the proper Action to achieve them.

To achieve your *dreams* you must *wake up* and take Action.

"Save the world from unfulfilled potential.  Take action on your dreams...now!" -Mr. Positive Dave Boufford

"It is time for us all to stand and cheer for the doer, the achiever - the one who recognizes the challenges and does something about it."
--Vince Lombardi, 1913-1970

"I never worry about action, only inaction."
-Winston Churchill, 1874-1965

"In the arena of human life the honors and rewards fall to those who show their good qualities in Action."
-Aristotle, 384BC-322BC

"People who are unable to motivate themselves must be content with mediocrity, no matter how impressive their other talents." -Andrew Carnegie, 1835-1919

"Forget past mistakes.  Forget failures.  Forget everything except what you're going to do now and do it."
-William Durant, 1861-1947

"Live Deliberately" – Greg Pinneo

## **CHAPTER 16 – MASTERY OF FEAR**

Fear is an extremely harmful emotion. Although not useless (on a primal level, it is good to have a fear of lions, tigers & bears) its benefits do not outweigh its drawbacks.

*We do not need fear; we need understanding.*

Napoleon Hill described the 6 basic fears with which every person is cursed: Poverty, Criticism, Loss of love, Ill health, Old age & Death. These are the most challenging to overcome.

There are an unlimited amount of other fears, all of which are a hindrance to your success. They must all be kept under control.

Realize that although Fear can never be completely eliminated, it must be controlled. Control your fears.

The definition of courage: Action in spite of fear.
Be courageous!

Real estate magnate Greg Pinneo suggests that you *break* your fear gauge and leave it that way - smashed, never to be repaired.

I have 3 suggestions for battling fear:

1. Face your Fears.
   Facing your fears is usually the best way to conquer them. (Be prepared and don't physically hurt yourself.)

2. Learn to understand the source your Fears.
   Many fears come from a lack of understanding. There is usually nothing to be afraid of. Learning more about something helps us become more comfortable with it. This can reduce or possibly eliminate certain Fears.

3. Do not think about your Fears.
   Think of your goals instead. Devote no time to thinking about your Fears. Do not let them into your Mind. We know that what you think about will happen, so do not think about your Fears.

There is a difference between being afraid and being precautionary. You want to take precautions. We addressed this in the chapter on Preparation. You want to be prepared. You want to know where you are going and have the tools needed for the job.

Being prepared reduces Fear.
When you are ready for the emergency, it is no longer something to Fear. When you are prepared, there is no need for Fear.

In "Deliberate Success," Pinneo challenges us to get out of our comfort zone. 'You do not live life in your comfort zone. Your comfort zone is where you rest and recover, not where you live. People are made to live.'

Are you a sailor if your boat stays tied to the dock? Your boat is safer tied to the dock, but it was *designed* for open waters. You were *designed* to Live.

"Always do what you are afraid to do."
-Ralph Waldo Emerson

"Have the courage to live. Anyone can die."
– Robert Cody

This is the *call to Action*. Get out of your comfort zone. *Live your life.*

"The only thing we have to fear is fear itself."-
Franklin D Roosevelt, – March 4, 1933

## CHAPTER 17 – MOMENTUM

Sir Isaac Newton's First Law of Motion states that a body at rest will stay at rest or a body in motion will stay in motion unless acted upon by an outside force. This is known as inertia.

Newton's First Law applies to people as well as objects.

People at rest tend to stay at rest unless acted on by an outside force. People in motion tend to stay in motion unless they encounter an obstacle.

Are you at rest or are you in motion? Are you waiting for someone or something to inspire you? Stop waiting for an outside force. Take Responsibility *and Action*. Make something happen. Life is short. Why spend time waiting for life to *happen* to you?

Once you set yourself in motion, you will stay in motion until an outside force gets in the way. Unfortunately for some people it does not take much of an outside force to stop their motion. Be Persistent in your Desire to stay on track.

In order to maintain the Momentum necessary to achieve your goals you need a burning Desire to achieve them. You need to find the *emotion* to make yourself unstoppable.

The laws of Inertia and Momentum apply to *everything*. They apply to your habits. Have you ever procrastinated starting an exercise routine? This procrastination becomes a habit. You will find that exercise gets easier and more enjoyable the more you do it. The new habit replaces the old habit. Momentum will maintain *either* habit. You decide which habits you want in your life.

This idea applies to your goals. They *must* become a part of your lifestyle. They must be *habitual*.

Habits are a product of inertia. It is a habit because you keep doing it. Some habits are hard to break because there is a lot of Momentum behind them. Your goal is to add Momentum to good habits.

Use emotional Affirmations to add Momentum to your Subconscious Mind.

Momentum is technically mass multiplied by velocity ($mv$).

We want our good habits to have a lot of Momentum. They need a lot of mass - or weight. They need a lot of velocity - or speed. Add weight – or importance – to your good habits. Reinforce your good habits and they will gain Momentum. As you keep repeating them, they will be more difficult to stop.

Once you get in the habit of eating right or exercising, it is much easier to maintain it.

Whatever your goals, they should maintain their Momentum through constant planning and constant *Action*.

In your pursuit of success you will encounter obstacles. There will be times that you feel that your path is blocked. This will reduce your Momentum.

At this point you must face the *Test of Persistence*.

## **CHAPTER 18 – PERSISTENCE**

Thomas Edison, the inventor of the electric light bulb failed over 10,000 times before finally figuring out how to make it work. Persistence was the key. He knew that eventually he would run out of things that did not work. In the end, his Subconscious Mind brought him the answer.

Persistence is the consistent pursuit of a Goal.

The process you choose to achieve your goal may be constant or it may be constantly changing. Planning and evaluation allows you to assess what needs to be done.

Clearly and emotionally impress the Goal upon your Subconscious Mind and keep your Momentum high.

### *Great Successes must pass the Test of Persistence.*

Great rewards only come after you apply Action and Persistence. Continue to impress your Goal upon your Subconscious Mind - *and keep going.*

Many people keep doing the same thing over and over and are confused why their results are always the same. Persistence does not mean simply repeating an action. You must be persistent about your goals, not necessarily about the specific process you have chosen to reach them.

Persistence should be a process of constantly tweaking your system to make it better and better. You must remain driven yet fluid and open to the possibility of altering your path to reach your goals. The Decision and Determination to continue toward your goal in spite of obstacles will require Adaptation as well as Persistence.

Learn from your mistakes, adapt, and go forward.

Napoleon Hill said that "Every failure holds the seed of equivalent success."

Each time something goes wrong, stop and think: why did this happen and what can I do differently to prevent it from happing again?  How can I adapt and overcome?

"When defeat comes, accept it as a signal that your plans are not sound. Rebuild those plans and set sail once more toward your coveted goal." -Napoleon Hill, 1883-1970

It is ok to make mistakes, just don't make the same mistakes twice.  If you are going to screw up, at least do it in a new and different way.
Learn and Adapt.

Was Thomas Edison a failure because he figured out 10,000 ways not to make a light bulb?

Fuel your goals with such a burning desire that no obstacle can stand in your way.  Use obstacles as a way to 'fuel your fire'.

"My advice is find fuel in failure. Sometimes failure gets you closer to where you want to be." -Michael Jordan

"Failure is simply the opportunity to begin again, this time more intelligently." – Henry Ford, 1863-1947

When something goes wrong, find the equivalent seed of success. Find the good in the situation. Find the positive side.

Success takes time. Realize that you must *build* a future. Overnight success is rare. Success takes Patience and Persistence.

"The greatest glory in living lies not in never falling, but in rising every time we fall." -Nelson Mandela

"Success is going from failure to failure without a loss of enthusiasm. " -Winston Churchill, 1874-1965

"It's not that I'm so smart, it's just that I stay with problems longer." -Albert Einstein, 1879-1955

"Always bear in mind that your own resolution to succeed is more important than any one thing."
-Abraham Lincoln, 1809-1865

"We must accept finite disappointment, but we must never lose infinite hope." -Martin Luther King, Jr.

"Success seems to be largely a matter of hanging on after others have let go. " -William Feather, 1889-1981

"Effort only fully releases its reward after a person refuses to quit. " -Napoleon Hill, 1883-1970

## **CHAPTER 19 - FAITH**
### "You Can Do it if you Believe You Can"

Anything is possible if you *visualize it* and *believe it*. Have Faith that this is true, and act accordingly. As you develop clarity of your Goals by *visualizing* them frequently, the *Belief* in your Vision will grow as well. Practice this daily.

Have Faith that your Persistence will bring results. Why keep doing something if you don't think it will actually make a difference?

In order to be a success you must have *Faith in yourself* - Faith in your decisions and in your abilities. Others will believe in you when you believe in yourself.

Practice having faith in yourself and in your decisions and you will develop Confidence. Confident people get more of what they want out of life. They get it because they expect to get it.

Have *Faith in others*. People will be good to you if you are good to them. Be trusting and forgiving. Have Faith that if you are true to your purpose, you will attract people who will help you. They will be drawn by the nature of your thought. Others will be willing you help you because you are willing to help others.

Believe in others and they will believe in you.

Have *Faith in the Universe*. For every action there is an equal and opposite reaction. Have Faith that it is true and act accordingly. Every action or inaction has a consequence. Have Faith in the Law of Attraction.

Have *Faith in God* (whatever *God* means to you) and an infinite intelligence that is greater than you. There are many secrets that lie outside of our Awareness.

Live in Faith and there will be no need to Fear. *Believe* and you will not Fear.

"Take the first step in Faith. You don't have to see the whole staircase, just take the first step."
- Dr. Martin Luther King Jr., 1929-1968

The Creator did not build a staircase to nowhere.
Take the next step up toward your goal.

"We must walk consciously only part way toward our goal, and then leap in the dark to our success."
-Henry David Thoreau, 1817-1962

"It is our duty to proceed as though the limits of our abilities do not exist."
-Pierre Teilhard de Chardin, 1881-1955

"If you believe, you will receive whatever you ask for…"
–Matthew 21:22

## **CHAPTER 20 - THANKFUL & GRATEFUL**

Be Thankful and Grateful for what you have.

Give thanks every day – for all that you have.

In the chapter on the Subconscious Mind you were reminded that your Subconscious Mind is working 24 hours a day, trying to help you achieve what you focus on. If you make it a habit to be Thankful and Grateful, your Subconscious Mind will continue to look for ways to bring those things into your life.

Anything you focus on will expand.

Focus on what you are Thankful for so that it will grow.

Some years ago I was going through tough times. I had a decent job but I was living paycheck-to-paycheck. My work life was not ideal, and I was not enjoying life the way I should have been. I made the decision to pray every day. Having a religious upbringing, I knew that a key ingredient of prayer was being Thankful for what I had. I decided to think about the things I was Thankful for. I was Thankful that my basic needs were met. I knew that the majority of people in the world are unable to enjoy what I considered the 'basics'. I realized that I was thankful for my house, my job, and my car. Without these things life would have been much more difficult.

Every day on the way to work I told myself that I was thankful for my house, my job, and my car. I did not have my dream house or my dream job or my dream car *but they all worked*. Every day for years I was thankful for these things. As time went on the list of things I was thankful for grew.

One day I was driving to work being thankful as I had been for the last 4 years: thankful for my house, my job, and my car – and I had a profound realization. I had 2 houses, my own successful business, and 2 cars. Four years prior, I had begun to remind myself of how Thankful & Grateful I was. Since that time, I had bought several investment properties, I started my own business, and I had purchased a beautiful new car. *What I was thankful for had more than doubled.*

*What you focus on expands. Energy flows where attention goes.*
Be thankful for what you have and it will grow.
Focus on what you do not want and it too will grow.

Albert Einstein noted that there are 2 ways to live life: One is by believing that *nothing is a miracle* and the other is by believing that *everything is a miracle.*

I grew up learning about the Bible. I remember hearing stories of miracles such as the parting of the Red Sea and remember thinking, 'Why don't these biblical miracles happen today? There must be some scientific explanation for the miracles we read about in the Bible.' At that time I was living my life as though *nothing were a miracle.*

As you practice being Thankful and Grateful you will start to realize that *everything is a miracle.*

How many blades of grass are in your yard? How many blades of grass are in your state? How many blades of grass are in the world? Their abundance is a miracle.

I am thankful for an abundant world.

Have you ever seen a weed or a flower growing from a crack in the concrete in the middle of a 6-lane highway? Isn't that a miracle? How does it happen?

What about clouds? Sure we can scientifically explain their existence. They are clumps of water vapor. Yet, aren't they a miracle?

Sunsets are one of my favorite miracles. Every day we have amazing natural light shows.

The human body is a miracle. Its adaptability, complexity and endurance are incredible. Your body works better the more you use it. Get in motion, take Action, and put it to use. Use it but do not abuse it. Be kind to your body and treat it right. You want to make the most of this miracle.

As you begin to practice being Thankful and Grateful you will learn not to take people and things for granted. You will start to realize that *everything is a miracle*.

*I am thankful to live in a world of miracles.*

## CHAPTER 21 – HAPPINESS

"Folks are generally as happy as they choose to be."
-Abraham Lincoln, 1809-1865

Most people are waiting for some outside influence to make them happy. Although we have all experienced when an outside influence makes us happy, these moments are often temporary.

**Happiness Comes from Within.**
No amount of external influence will continuously sustain happiness in our lives.

You need to *decide* to be happy and *be happy*. The best way to do this is to think about what you are Thankful and Grateful for on a daily basis.

The best things in life do not cost money. Think of the things or times in your life that make you truly happy. Often you will find the source of your happiness does not require money.

Think of the things that really make you happy and be Thankful for them.

A happy attitude will yield happy results. Be happy towards others and others will be happy towards you.

*You will become what you think about* so think about being happy.

Some people, either consciously or subconsciously, live their life trying to gain the respect or appreciation of someone else. They think that this will make them happy. If you have been trying to gain the approval of someone specific who still does not appreciate you, you need to realize that it is likely that they never will. Their approval should not be a source of happiness for you. Find a new source of happiness that is not dependent on an external source. Happiness is internal.

You cannot change other people, only they can change themselves. Change yourself and be ready to help when others are ready to change.

Happiness comes from achieving goals. This is another reason why goals are important. **Goals are a source of happiness**. Most people are happiest while on the journey towards reaching a goal. It is important to have new goals before you reach your current goals. This will keep you in a constant state of motion, growth, achievement and happiness. Most people are happiest in a state of anticipation and growth.

"Happiness is not in the mere possession of money; it lies in the joy of achievement, in the thrill of creative effort."
–Franklin D. Roosevelt, 1882-1945

"The basic thing is that everyone wants happiness, no one wants suffering. And happiness mainly comes from our own attitude, rather than from external factors. If your own mental attitude is correct, even if you remain in a hostile atmosphere, you feel happy."
– Tenzin Gyatso, the (14th) Dalai Lama

"Learn to enjoy every minute of your life. Be happy now. Don't wait for something outside of yourself to make you happy in the future. Think how really precious is the time you have to spend, whether it's at work or with your family. Every minute should be enjoyed and savored."
--Earl Nightingale, 1921-1989

"Happiness is anyone and anything at all that's loved by you." –Charlie Brown

"Success is getting what you want. Happiness is wanting what you get. "-Dale Carnegie, 1888-1955

"Happiness is when what you think, what you say, and what you do are in harmony."
–Mohandas Gandhi, 1869-1948

"Happiness is not by chance, but by choice."
-Jim Rohn

"That man is richest whose pleasures are cheapest."
–Henry David Thoreau, 1817-1862

"Very little is needed to make a happy life. It is all within yourself, in your way of thinking. "
-Marcus Aurelius, 121-180

"Happiness depends on ourselves."
–Aristotle, 384BC-322BC

Just try smiling more.

## CHAPTER 22 – HEALTH & WEALTH

The concepts of Health and Wealth are presented together because their achievement requires following several of the same guidelines: You must set Goals; you must have Discipline, Determination, Persistence, and Faith in yourself; and you must have *Self Control*.

Having good health and wealth will dramatically improve your chances of success. The Principles in this book will help you achieve health and wealth. In turn, health and wealth will help you live a life that embodies all of the Principles.

Living a life of good health is living in pursuit of your potential. The human body is amazing. Many people do not put it to the test. You should test yourself to see what heights your body is capable of. There is so much more you can do when you apply yourself.

Feeling healthy makes it easier to feel happy.

Being healthy and fit is part of your preparation for life. Each day you go out into the world and out of your comfort zone. You want to be in a body that is ready for the adventures ahead.

Your body is one tool that will be with you for the entire journey. Take care of your body and elevate your life.

Everything we put in our bodies affects our health.
- Food
- Drinks
- Drugs

A case could be made for or against every piece of food that we eat, beverage we drink or drug that we take:
- Some people are vegetarians and do not eat meat.
- Some people are particular about their water.
- Some people prefer only organic products.
- Some people have allergies.
- Some people take over the counter medication.
- Some people use natural healing.
- Some people feel they will die without their prescriptions- others actually will.

Everyone is different and has to do what is right for them. Listen to your body; it will tell you what it needs.

## The MIKE WAY: Living a Healthy Life

Diets do not work in the long run. This is because they are approached as non-permanent. When people go on a diet, they are "on a diet" implying that there is an alternative: "Going off the diet". Any time you are "on a diet" you always run the risk of going "off the diet". Maybe you are on a diet in order to get to a certain weight, and then you plan to go off the diet thinking that by some miracle you will maintain the new weight by going back to your old habits. There are no diets - Just lifestyles. I recommend living a healthy one.

**Here are my Recommendations for Living a Healthy Life:**

- **Minimize your fat and caloric intake.**

  Read the label to see how much fat and calories are in the products that you intend to eat. If you make this a habit you will learn which foods have less fat than others. Eating unnecessary fat will make you fat.

- **Minimize your intake of fried food. It is full of fat.**

  I know it tastes good; save it for a special occasion.

- **Do not eat fast food. It is also full of fat and calories.**

  Have a deli sandwich or salad instead.

- **Get regular exercise.**

  If you eat more calories than you burn, you will add fat. Therefore you must burn calories by engaging in an exercise of choice.

- **Exercise with your objective in mind.**

  Exercise can be divided into 2 main categories: Aerobic activity & Weight lifting. Many exercises are a combination of the two. Aerobic activity will burn fat as well as increase your stamina, blood flow, and energy level. It also stretches your muscles and increases flexibility. Lifting weights will build muscle, which improves strength & tone as well as consuming fat. Exercise will increase your energy levels and build confidence.

  Aerobic Activities – Choose what makes you feel good.
  - Sports – basketball, volleyball, tennis, etc.
  - Swimming
  - Bike riding, walking, jogging, running, hiking
  - Aerobics, dancing

  See www.BeachBody.com for more ideas

Weight Lifting – Choose your target muscle area then select the method that best targets that muscle group. Barbells, dumbbells, and weight machines are commonly used tools. There are hundreds of techniques and combinations. See www.MensHealth.com & www.WomensHealthMag.com for more information.

- **Read articles about food and nutrition.**
  Learn what is best for you. Everyone is different. There are dietary supplements that can help you achieve your goals.
- **Eat fresh fruits and vegetables.** They are *good* for you.
- **Eat proper amounts of vitamins and minerals.**
- **Alcohol should only be consumed in moderation.**
- **Do not *worry*. Worrying causes stress.**
  In the chapter about your Subconscious Mind, we briefly addressed the dangers of worrying. I bring it up again here because it is a health issue. I hear so many people say, "I am so stressed out" or "I'm having such a stressful day." I always respond by asking the question, "Do you know what causes stress?" Obviously they don't otherwise they would not be stressed. *Stress is caused by worrying.* Do not worry and do not stress.

  If you find yourself in a stressful situation, most often the situation requires a *decision* that needs to be made. Make that decision and move on. Stop worrying and lead a stress-free life.

- **Drink Xango® every day.**

   Xango® is a delicious health beverage made from Mangosteen fruit. The Mangosteen fruit – especially the rind- is rich with nutrients and antioxidants. It has been used for centuries to treat a variety of health conditions. Awareness of the Mangosteen has been limited because it does not grow outside tropical areas and does not travel well. Today, its health benefits and deliciousness are more readily available. The Mangosteen juices with the greatest health benefits are those made from the rind of the fruit. Xango® is one such product.

   Xango® can also be the key to both health and wealth. Go to www.FeelingSuperGood.com to learn more. Call 800-360-5914 for a free CD.


In order to be healthy and wealthy you must exercise Self-Control. You will not achieve your goals without Self-Control.


Health is one form of wealth. Wealth is *well-being* and can be defined in many ways. If you are looking for wealth in monetary terms than follow the Principles of this book.

Since we know that *you get what you give*, we know that the extent of your Service, both *quality and quantity*, will determine the extent of your reward. Determining the type of wealth you seek should determine the type of service you will render.

Some people believe that success is not related to money. That may be true - although money can help increase our *level* of success. It also better enables us to help other people. Increasing your ability to help others should be a part of your success strategy.

I like Robert Kiyosaki's definition of wealth: Wealth is the length of time you can maintain your current lifestyle without working. If you quit working tomorrow, how long could you live without adjusting your lifestyle? That is how wealthy you are. Are you 1 week wealthy? 1 year wealthy?

Maintaining your lifestyle without working can happen in one of two ways: Savings & Passive Income.

If you can maintain your current lifestyle forever without working then you are *infinitely wealthy*. How is that possible? It is possible with passive income. There are a lot of ways to earn passive income. Interest income is passive income. If you have $1 million in the bank at 6% interest, you have monthly payments from this interest of $5,000. If you can happily live off of $5,000 per month then you are *infinitely wealthy*.

On the other hand, if you live off just savings of $1 million without any interest, you will run out of money in 200 months (16 years).

To learn about passive income, read *Rich Dad, Poor Dad, Cashflow Quadrant,* or *Retire Young, Retire Rich* by Robert Kiyosaki.

## **CHAPTER 23 – A PLEASING PERSONALITY**

This chapter can be summarized in a single sentence:
**Take a sincere interest in other people.** If you can do this,
you will have a pleasing personality.

An important key in mastering this habit is to remember
people's names. If you can do this one thing, you will be
wildly popular and successful in almost any field of work
you choose. It is difficult to take a sincere interest in other
people if you do not remember their names.

Another suggestion is to avoid arguing with others. If you
must disagree, do it tactfully & respectfully.
Most of us can think of times when we hear somebody say
something that we know to be false. It takes some self-
control to restrain yourself and maintain your composure,
but it is worth practicing.

Dale Carnegie's book *How to Win Friends and Influence
People* is a great resource for mastering the habit of a
pleasing personality.

You get what you give. Take interest in others and others
will take interest in you. Be nice, courteous, generous, and
kind to others and you will get the same in return.

## CHAPTER 24 – TOLERANCE

Not everyone is just like you. Learn to appreciate the views and opinions of others. Diversity adds great value to the world. New ideas come rapidly when different people work together in a spirit of harmony. Be open-minded.

When someone views something differently than you, practice tolerance and remember reality bubbles. Why is their reality different than yours? It is challenging but rewarding to understand the perspectives and realities of other people.

We must be tolerant and accepting of other's views and beliefs. I do not have the same beliefs as everyone else, nor do you. It is impossible to agree with everyone but remember: You will get what you give every time. It is not worth argument and animosity; you will get argument and animosity in return. Do not argue with others. Seek to understand their point of view. If you still disagree then keep it to yourself. Arguing will most likely not get you what you want out of a situation.

It is not your place to judge others. Your reality bubble is much too small to have adequate knowledge of the 'truth' to accurately judge others.

The Actions of others will cause their own rewards or punishment. Stay focused on your own success and you will be too busy to criticize others.

"Judge not, that you be not judged. For with the judgment you pronounce you will be judged, and the measure you give will be the measure you get." – Matthew 7:1-2

Intolerance is poison for your Subconscious Mind.

## **CHAPTER 25 - TRUST**

You will get what you give.
Trust others and others will trust you.

Trust yourself first, and then trust others.

When your trust is violated it is easy to feel hurt.
This is a crucial time to make good decisions and to forgive.

People who lie, cheat, and steal are only hurting themselves. This is why it so easy to forgive them. They think about lying, cheating and stealing. Therefore, they attract it into their lives. Because of this, people lie, cheat, and steal from them. These actions are perpetuated because of their Momentum.

Avoid these types of thoughts and stay positive. Feelings of hatred and revenge will only hurt you. Stay positive and continue to attract positive people and things.

Make it a habit to carry a $100 bill with you at all times. Carrying $100 with you at all times will teach your Subconscious Mind two very important things: Trust yourself and Trust others. You can trust yourself to not spend $100. You can trust other people to not take your $100. This exercise is worth much more than the value of the money. Set aside one $100 bill in your wallet or purse and leave it there. Maybe one day you'll be glad you had it, but if you do use it you must replace it right away. This is not an exercise in spending. It's an exercise in Trust & Self-Control. If $100 does not move your gauge then try $1000.

## CHAPTER 26 – COOPERATION

Success comes from relationships.

We need other people to be successful. We are interdependent of each other. The sooner you embrace this, the sooner you will become a success. We need to work with others. Understanding Reality Bubbles in Chapter 7 will aid in your ability to work with others.

We need other people. Think about it:
You get up in the morning and brush your teeth.
Did you make the toothpaste?
You get dressed. Did you make your clothes?
You put on your shoes. Did you make them?
You eat your breakfast.
Did you milk the cow? Gather the eggs?
Squeeze the juice? Bake the bread?
You look at your watch and drive to work.
Did you make your watch? Did you build your own car?
You can't get very far without other people.

"The quality of your life is the quality of your relationships." -Anthony Robbins

## THE IMPORTANCE OF YOUR NETWORK

Your network creates your net worth.

Who you know and surround yourself with has everything to do with your success. This is partially because a larger network increases your ability to help and serve others.

We have all been in situations where we require the help of other people. If you can easily access people who can help you (and truly want to because you have or would readily help them) you have increased your efficiency. Readily available help makes life a lot easier and much more enjoyable. If you are always ready to help others, others will always be ready to help you.

Learn to cooperate with others in a spirit of harmony and you will be successful. It's great when people can work together and get along. When you are able to achieve a true spirit of harmony then the magic of the Mind begins to shine.

When people are working together in a spirit of harmony, their Subconscious Minds harmonize as well, producing positive new energy. New ideas come forth that would never have been considered by one individual. There is power in numbers, especially if everyone is working together in a spirit of harmony.

A successful leader takes this concept even further.

## CHAPTER 27 - LEADERSHIP

Leaders set the example.

Those seeking success in any terms should study the qualities of Leadership even if they do not specifically supervise anyone. Set an example for yourself and *be the person you intend to become.*

Those seeking success in terms of growing a business or advancing up the corporate ladder will use additional characteristics and skills beyond the 30 Principles of Success covered in this book. They will require developing the characteristics and skills of a Leader.

A good leader generally:

- Is responsible
- Plans for the future
- Sets attainable goals and achieves them
- Takes Initiative and decisive Action
- Teaches and helps develop others
- Thinks rationally, clearly and carefully
- Knows their job and is technically proficient
- Practices Self Confidence and Self Control
- Strives for constant self and team improvement
- Adapts to circumstances and overcomes obstacles
- Reaches good decisions quickly & stands by them
- Develops and initiates teamwork and cooperation
- Exercises self and team discipline
- Sets an example
- Communicates well and keeps others informed
- Follows through on expectations
- Looks out for the best interest of everyone involved
- Is Fair and Consistent in their actions

Good leaders not only understand the Principle of Cooperation, but they master the practice of Delegation and Follow-Through. Delegation is more than just 'telling people what to do'. Someone who is good at delegating follows up and makes sure expectations are met. They guide others and make sure the job gets done. Good leaders give constructive feedback on weak points, praise positives, and adapt as needed based on progress.

Even if you have a small business with no employees, you will still need leadership skills for your business to be successful. You need to demonstrate leadership over yourself and take initiative. You need to lead your suppliers, partners, and supporters to see your vision.

Believe in yourself if you want others to believe in you. Leaders calmly, rationally and confidently demonstrate decisiveness.

"Management is doing things right; leadership is doing the right things." -Peter F. Drucker, 1909-2005

"You cannot lead others where you are not willing to go." -Dr. Steven Foster

"The quality of a leader is reflected in the standards they set for themselves."
- Ray Kroc, Founder of McDonalds, 1902-1984

"If your actions inspire others to dream more, learn more, do more and become more, you are a leader. "
-John Quincy Adams, 6th U.S. President, 1767-1848

## CHAPTER 28
## DISCIPLINE: TIME & MONEY MANAGEMENT

*Time is the great equalizer.* Everyone has the same amount of time in the day. No matter how rich and successful you become, you cannot create more time.

All of the Principles in this book are worthy of your attention, but without time management you will not be as effective as possible.

Have a system to prioritize and organize.
Which task is most important?
Which tasks are immediate priorities?

In *The 7 Habits of Highly Effective People*, Stephen Covey gives two great lessons in time management. Covey discusses ones sphere of influence and sphere of concern. It is futile to expend a lot of effort and energy on things that concern you but you have no influence over. This is known as worrying. *Worrying is useless.* Do not worry.

Covey also urges readers to evaluate tasks according to their urgency and importance. Many people focus too much time and energy on supposedly 'urgent' but essentially unimportant things.

Many time management systems and planners are available; choose a system that works for you. No matter what system you choose, you need a planner or management system. Get and Stay Organized!

Just like goals, you will be more likely to finish daily tasks if they are written down.

Maintain a healthy balance between family, work and play.

Enjoy your job. If you do not, change your situation so that you do.

People who enjoy their jobs are successful because time is spent working and 'playing' at the same time. This makes achieving a balance much easier, and certainly more mentally and emotionally healthy.

Most people spend their time working for a wage or salary. Your income is the result of how you spend your time. Spend your time wisely. Often, money *is* an important part of achieving goals, so proper money management is imperative.

Figure out where your money is going.
Cash is good but *Cash Flow* is more important.
Ask yourself: Where does my money come from and where does it go?

Here are some basic money management tips:

1. Figure out where your money *comes from* and determine what changes need to be made.

   In most cases, your amount of income is determined by the amount of Responsibility you have and the quality and quantity of Service you provide. If you want more money, think about ways to take on more Responsibility and ways to provide greater quality and quantity of Service.

2. Figure out where your money *goes* and determine what changes need to be made.

3. Track your expenses.
   Examine them at least once a month.
   Make necessary adjustments.

To successfully manage your money you need to understand your *Income Statement*. It tracks your Income and Expenses. What is coming in and what is going out? Income – Expenses = Profit.

In order to successfully manage your money you should also understand *Balance Sheets*. They track your Assets & Liabilities. For a great introduction to financial literacy please read Robert Kiyosaki's bestseller *Rich Dad, Poor Dad*. Here Kiyosaki explains the difference between Assets and Liabilities.

- Assets feed you.
- Liabilities eat you.

Since time is limited and money is not, we can establish that time is more valuable than money.

If this is not yet the case in your life, then you need to determine: How much is your time worth? Now think of ways to increase that amount.

Have a system to keep track of your money. There are a lot of software programs available for financial management. You can use charts. You can hire a financial advisor. You can hire a bookkeeper.

Read T. Harv Eker's *Secrets of the Millionaire Mind* for a simple yet effective money management system.

Whatever system you choose, saving must be part of your plan. Saving helps develop Discipline and Self Control. It demonstrates *Responsibility* through Self Control.

The universe rewards responsibility. Be responsible with your money and it will grow.

Systems to manage your time and money will increase your effectiveness to a great extent. Devote time to putting these systems in place and you will accelerate your success.

## CHAPTER 29 – RISK & REWARD

Risk and reward are like cause and effect.

An action causes a reaction.  A risk causes a reward.

The greater the risk, the greater the reward can be.  Risk also implies a probability of failure; therefore, each risk needs to be calculated to keep the probability of failure to a minimum.

Many people want to keep their risks to a minimum.

This is understandable, although they will also keep their rewards to a minimum.  Take the risk to receive the reward.

A turtle must come out of his shell in order to go somewhere.

A boat is safer in the harbor, but that is not where it is meant to be.

Statistically, one of the riskiest things a person can do is to get in a car, yet we do so all of the time.  Another great risk is depending on job security, yet many people do this as well.  Job security is something that has become a myth in the new millennium.  Relying on job security is risky.

Given that these two risky activities are so very common, new risks should not seem so scary.

Every Action or Inaction has some degree of Risk.

Live a *deliberate life* and choose your risks.

Everything you do is a risk that will generate a return.

Since you are going to be doing 'something' anyway, shouldn't it be something *deliberate*?

*Live your life* and *go outside of your comfort zone.*
You do not grow in your comfort zone.
You do not learn in your comfort zone.
Step outside of your comfort zone and *make it habitual.*

"The person who gets the farthest is generally the one who is willing to do and dare." – Dale Carnegie

"We must all suffer from one of two pains: the pain of discipline or the pain of regret. The difference is discipline weighs ounces while regret weighs tons. "-Jim Rohn

"You will either step forward in growth or you will step back into safety." -Abraham Maslow

"Anyone who has never made a mistake has never tried anything new." -Albert Einstein

## CHAPTER 30 – THE DESIRE TO LEARN MORE

Constantly build your Knowledge and expand your Awareness.

Be confident of your competence. Be technically proficient with the tools and language of your chosen field. Greater knowledge increases your probability of success.

In *The 7 Habits of Highly Effective People* Steven Covey describes the 7th Habit of "Sharpening the Saw". This is the desire to continue to learn your trade in spite of your current level of proficiency.

The most successful people are constantly learning, and continue to do so every day.

"There is nothing noble in being superior to some other person. True nobility comes from being superior to your previous self." -Hindu Proverb

You must keep constantly improving, both mentally and physically. Be in a constant state of growth, movement and change for the better.

"Anyone who stops learning is old, whether at twenty or eighty. Anyone who keeps learning stays young. The greatest thing in life is to keep your Mind young."
-Henry Ford, 1863-1947

The world is constantly changing. You may have been an expert yesterday, but are you the expert of tomorrow?

Thanks for reading the 30 Principles of Success. I sincerely hope that you found some new insights that will change the way you *live your life*. I have met many people that seem one step away from learning one of these principles but fail to embody and apply them. Some Principles in the book were lessons that I needed to learn and witness repeatedly before I understood their timeless consistency.

If you've read this far then you have an interest in improving your life and the world around you. Use these Principles. Treat others as you wish to be treated. Give generously with the knowledge and Faith that you will undeniably receive an equal and opposite reaction. Increase your *Service*, for it will reward you and make the world a better place.

In this book I made a deliberate attempt to avoid lengthy discussion about religion. The 30 Principles work regardless of your personal religious beliefs. To my knowledge, these Principles are not inconsistent with any religious teachings. Although a relationship with God will bring these principles to an entirely new level, they will still work regardless of your secular or spiritual beliefs.

This book is brief and I make no claim that it is the comprehensive guide to success, however I think you'll find that the tools are here to live the life of your dreams.

Read this book often and apply the Principles one by one. Some will be easier than others. Devote time to developing the Principles that need improvement in your life.

Go forth taking responsibility and acting appropriately.

Be mindful that *you will get what you give* and act accordingly. Be conscious of your Awareness and expand it constantly. Develop Affirmations that will steer your Mind in the direction of your Goals. Visualize those goals *clearly* and take actions based on your Faith that they will be achieved. Think only of what you want, or want for others. Keep your thoughts on your positive future. Appreciate the present. Be Thankful for all you have. Conduct yourself in a way that will attract the collaboration of other people. Project an attitude that you would be happy to receive in return. Seek an understanding of other people. Think of ways to inspire them. Imagine possibilities and focus on your Goals. Enjoy the abundant world of miracles around you. Take charge of yourself and get everything organized. Get your plans in place then *take Action*! Observe your progress and be adaptable. Stay true to your purpose and have Faith that the world is on your side. Be happy and *enjoy the ride!* Take care of yourself. Appreciate others and take interest in their lives. Be patient with other people and tolerant with those who do not believe as you do. Trust yourself. Trust others. Trust the Universe and take *Action* when opportunities arise. Work with others in a spirit of harmony. Stay at the top of your game and always give your best. Love your Life and enjoy everything in it. And remember that…
 *You will become what you think about.*
 I sincerely wish you the best.


 Go to www.FeelingSuperGood.com to continue the journey and fully embrace the Philosophy into your life.

## SOME SOURCES OF MY INSPIRATION

### BOOKS

| | |
|---|---|
| Dale Carnegie | How to Win Friend & Influence People |
| Stephen Covey | The 7 Habits of Highly Effective People |
| T. Harv Eker | Secrets of the Millionaire Mind |
| Michael Gerber | The E-Myth series of books |
| Napoleon Hill | Think and Grow Rich |
| | The Law of Success |
| | Success Through PMA |
| Robert Kiyosaki | Rich Dad, Poor Dad |
| | Retire Young, Retire Rich |
| | The Cashflow Quadrant |
| Watty Piper | The Little Engine That Could |
| Wallace Wattles | The Science of Getting Rich |

### AUDIO

| | |
|---|---|
| Jack Canfield | Teachers of the Secret |
| Greg Pinneo | Deliberate Success |
| Earl Nightingale | Lead the Field |
| | The Strangest Secret |
| Bob Proctor | Teachers of the Secret |
| Dolf De Roos | Wealth Magnet |

### FILM

| | |
|---|---|
| Ronda Byrne | The Secret |
| James Arthur Ray | Quantum Creations |

## RECOMMENDED WEBSITES

www.FeelingSuperGood.com
www.Supergood365.com
www.SuperGoodProducts.com
www.Nightingale-Conant.com
www.RichDad.com
www.MotivationInAMinute.com
www.MrPositive.com
www.SimpleTruths.com
www.ThinkTQ.com
www.TUT.com
www.TheSecret.tv
www.BobProctor.com
www.JamesRay.com
www.StephenCovey.com
www.PowerWithin.com
www.ReachReturns.com
www.MensHealth.com
www.WomensHealthMag.com
www.BeachBody.com
www.LifeIsGood.com

# ABOUT THE AUTHOR

Mike Swanson is an active consultant, coach, entrepreneur, investor and Realtor in Bellingham, WA. His travels regularly include Colorado & Las Vegas.

Mike graduated with a Business degree from the University of Colorado at Boulder.

For more about Mike go to www.FeelingSuperGood.com

Call 360-676-1591 or 800-360-5914 for any questions about *Living in the Pursuit of Your Potential* or to set up personal coaching or business consultations.

**www.FeelingSuperGood.com**

Thanks to Richard for sparking the idea to write this book.
Thanks to God for helping me to write it and finish it.
Thanks to Mom for unending support and encouragement.
Thanks to Dad for your input, insights and ideas.
Thanks to Kristine for your suggestions and encouragement.
Thanks to Dave for the great suggestions and perspective.
Thanks to Carissa for the graphic assistance.
Thanks to Dave Boufford for your encouragement & quotes.
Thanks to Greg Pinneo for the inspiration & education.
Thanks to Barbara Evans for your support and editing.

Quotes from Lead the Field, The Strangest Secret, Money
Magnet and Think and Grow Rich used courtesy of
Nightingale-Conant.
Quotes from The Secret used courtesy of TS Production.
Quotes from Robert Kiyosaki used courtesy of
Grand Central Publishing.
Quotes from Napoleon Hill used courtesy of
Highroads Media, Inc.

Made in the USA